FIRST & LAST
SONGS

FIRST & LAST SONGS

*a*lan *r*iach

CHAPMAN

ACKNOWLEDGEMENTS
A number of these poems have appeared in the following periodicals and books:
The Journal of New Zealand Literature, Landfall, Printout, Sport, Takahe, Lines Review, Gairfish and *Verse*; *The Literary Half-Yearly* (India), *Textures* (South Africa); *New Writing Scotland 8: The Day I Met the Queen Mother*, edited by Hamish Whyte and Janice Galloway (Aberdeen, Association for Scottish Literary Studies, 1990), *The Flinders Jubilee Anthology*, edited by Annie Greet and Syd Harrex (Flinders, South Australia, Centre for Research in the New Literatures in English, 1991), *Poetry New Zealand* 3, edited by Elizabeth Smither and Brian Turner (Auckland, Brick Row/Nagare, 1991) and *Poetry New Zealand* 10, edited by Alistair Paterson (Auckland, Brick Row, 1995). An earlier version of 'Common Language' was published in *Lifestories: Other Voices* 3, edited by Ruth and Oz Kraus (Auckland, Brick Row/Hallard Press, 1993). 'At Arrowhead' and 'The Canyon' were written after a journey across the United States in September 1993, made at the invitation of the American Embassy and the United States Information Agency, and organised by the Institute of International Education. I am very grateful to all those who made that journey possible.

Published by
CHAPMAN
4 Broughton Place
Edinburgh EH1 3RX
Scotland

A catalogue record for this volume is available from the British Library.

ISBN 0-906772-71-0

Chapman New Writing Series
Editor Joy Hendry
ISSN 0953-5306

Cover illustration: John Cunningham, from *Still Life with Music Stand*, 1016 x 914mm, oil on canvas.

Printed by GP Print, Wellington, New Zealand

Contents

1 Family

Beside the Arbia, in the moist woods, and in the dry scrub of the hillsides, I lay and felt the old security. A mole came burrowing up through the grass at my side, the jays swung on the branches overhead, and the snakes swished and glinted through last year's leaves. I walked in safety through dark tunnels among the broom and felt the night protect me. The currents of my life flowed together and swept me along. I wish their stream might have been more productive of human good, less costly in lives.

We get little help from others in living. What we learn from them are mostly the inessentials of life — tricks and skills. But occasionally we exchange obscure signals. They are reassurances that others face or have faced the same difficulties, problems, choices. That they react to the same stimuli, feel the same joy and anguish, make the same sort of shifts to deal with foreknowledge of mortality. We may record the past for various reasons: because we find it interesting; because by setting it down we can deal with it more easily; because we wish to escape from the prison where we face our individual problems, wrestle with our particular temptations, triumph in solitude and in solitude accept defeat and death. Autobiography is an attempted jail-break. The reader tunnels through the same dark.

— Stuart Hood, *Carlino*

Grant, repeating Mr Tallisker's speech on comparative heavens, said that the Gaels were the only race who visualised Heaven as a country of the young; which was endearing of them.

'They are the only known race who have no word for no,' said Laura drily. 'That is a much more revealing characteristic than their notions of eternity.'

— Josephine Tey, *The Singing Sands*

FROM FLINDERS, SOUTH AUSTRALIA, DRIFTS
ANOTHER SCENT OF DISTANCE

'The perfume drifted out upon the waters,'
my father (he was first mate on a Clanline
cargo vessel manned by lascars bound
for Sydney) told me, &
'We couldn't go in, though we wanted to
go in, it looked so
sunny & the trees were
dancing silver on the skyline &
the green leaves & the green grass shimmering.'

Adelaide, or Lisbon?
For now I can't remember
which route it was he would have taken, & know
I make a fiction of it all, like this.

Standing among the trees at Bedford Park,
looking past the bluegums down the hollow of the ranges,
to where the city stretches, over the wide estuarial plain,
low below a hovering cloud of blue polluted air,
I can breathe the scent coming out of the places around me,
& make of it this fiction I believe: I can
watch it go in colours from these Flinders ranges
drifting down the howe towards Adelaide's broad streets,
its stone-built buildings, pleasant & relaxing in the sun,
& out upon the waters where I do not know
my father may have passed, so long ago.

NOCTURNE

All I remember now is that shed, the wood,
   the saw, the shield, the paraffin lamp.
From distance like the place we lived in,
         his departure seemed
  like sudden disregard: he'd go
out, into a night of pelting rain, walk down
      the stone staircase, into & across
   the stone backyard, into
      that wooden shed —
& I would watch him from the kitchen window
small as a mouse then, innocent as toffee.
    But that's a memory rationalised
   by time & movement, placed
  as a painting, true
  in its vision, false
  in its frame.
What I remember that matters is this:
    the paraffin lamp
  a colour of gold
     no other expertise has given me
 no sense of what it means to see through light
 comes close to this:
     an old man making shapes with wood
bringing down the fragile glass
  thistle-headed mantle on the wick, & casting
  everything into a light of possibility
  achieved,
    unrelieved,
     amber sustained,
& a voice that was nothing but kindness.

A SHORT INTRODUCTION TO MY UNCLE JOHN

Nulla placere diu, neque vivere carmina possunt,
quae scribuntur aquae potoribus.

My Uncle John kept corks.
He kept the corks out of all the bottles of wine that were drunk in his
      apartment.
He kept them in a wickerwork basket, a laundry basket,
high as your thigh. It was two-thirds full
of corks. Oh, he had a use for them. He's
an artist; he paints pictures, portraits, landscapes,
mainly in oils. Over each painting on the walls of his studio
there's a light shining down, and he'd put two corks
under the frame of each painting at the bottom, just to
bring it out that extra inch from the wall,
so that the light wouldn't strike the glass directly.
But there were only so many paintings in the studio.
And there are always more bottles of good wine to draw
corks out of.
      Well, one day my Uncle John's wife Yvonne
discovered this laundry basket and saw
how it was two-thirds full of corks. They hadn't
been married long and John hadn't told her before
that he kept corks. So she thought up a way
to get rid of the corks, because,
really, what is a grown man doing
with a laundry basket two-thirds full
of corks?
      In their kitchen there's a window
that opens out onto the garden. Except that
their kitchen, studio and the whole apartment is on the top floor
of Albany Mansions at Charing Cross in Glasgow,
and the building itself curves around Charing Cross,
so the garden, which is tucked in, inside the curve or the V of the
      building,
is deep down there in a concrete canyon.
It gets very little light all day
and it's usually covered in a thick layer of soot and grime

and the air is often dense with exhaust fumes and other
exhalations of the city not conducive to
vegetable growth. Nevertheless, my Uncle John has taken pains
in gardening this little plot. He has planted
many things and hoped that they would grow,
even almost rushing downstairs to replant in the afternoon
the plants that he'd planted that morning, to get
the afternoon light on them, as it shifted in the shadows of the
     buildings.
               Anyway,
this window in their kitchen on the top floor of the building was
     opened by
being lifted *up* before it was swung *back*, into the room, on its
hinges on its left-hand side. So, Yvonne devised a plan to get rid of
     the corks.

She left the window open in the summer, just a little,
before they went to work, John to teach at the Art School,
and Yvonne to an estate agent's. She wedged a single cork in between
the window-frame and the lintel, and left it there.
Now, when it got cool in the evening after they were home from their
     work,
they would have to lift the window an inch before swinging it back
to close the frame flush with the lintel, and,
when they did that, the cork would fall
out of the niche it was wedged in, and into the dark canyon of the
     garden below,
where it would be lost, forever.
Yvonne began doing this one Tuesday morning.
It took until Thursday. On
Thursday evening she came home to find
John, already sitting there, at
the kitchen table, writing a letter, and having a glass of wine.
She noticed something out of the corner of her eye
over at the kitchen window,
so she went over to have a look.
And what she saw was this: the cork
was just as she'd left it that morning, wedged
between the frame and the lintel, but firmly stuck in
to the cork was a small pin. Attached to the

pin was a thread, which stretched down and around to the wooden
        panelling
next to the pantry door, where it was securely tied to a second small
        pin,
which was in its turn stuck tightly in
to the wood.
        'What,'
Yvonne said, 'is this?'
(When they closed the window now, the cork would fall, attached to its
        thread,
daintily, back into the kitchen, and dangle there between
the window-frame and the doorway, waiting and ready for use again
when the time came next morning.)
                'Ah yes,' my Uncle John replied, glancing round:
        'I rigged that up
just this afternoon. I was
losing
too many corks.'

THE FINGER

The Avenue goes over the hill, bisects
the University, and down to the lights at
Byres Road. On the left corner, there,
there's a wedge of building; everyone knew
the pub at the foot of Gilmore Hill, by
the nurses' flats: the Rubaiyat: two narrow
bars, one carpeted, each thick
with smoke & conversation, nurses, students.

One time I was late to reach the flat & found them
standing in the vestibule in coats, deliberating mightily
on what to do: Jim & Edward didn't believe
that I'd know where to go to meet them; Chris knew
I'd have known. He wanted to
go there directly, leaving a note in the letterbox, saying:
'The moving finger writes. . . .'
& it was the look on their faces, two of
shock & one
of satisfaction, when I said
'Sure. You'd have been in the Rubaiyat.'

— The mirrors in the bar were bevelled, pictures carved in silver
on them, verses from the sequence, masterworks of some forgotten period,
memorable as Fitzgerald, just as outmoded, inauthentic (of course)
— but what was to come
was Gillespie.

      My Uncle John & I
were passing, driving along Byres Road towards
a deli for a particular thing, & saw it, no longer
what it had been but a shell of stone with new wood round it.
We went in. There was somebody still serving beer. We had some.
What happened? we asked & were told of the takeover.
And the mirrors? Those bevelled Persian cavaliers,
the swirling scripted verses, silver on the smoky glass?
— were gone. And no great loss in honesty,

          but two weeks later, passing again,
driving towards the delicatessen again,
we saw the Merc pull up outside the bar.
The numberplate read GILLESPIE 1, and the man who got out
was the man: smug, plump, wristwatched with silver,
suited in sharkskin grey, hair thinned: it could be no other.

So my Uncle John & I nodded, said nothing, knew
that we had to do just what we had to do:

John parked the car. We got out & walked over
& opened the corner-swing doors of the pub
that had one time been the Rubaiyat, John holding open
the right-hand door, & I on the left, looking in
to see the man, now sitting down & facing us at the door,
at a bright wooden table waiting his lunch,
& now looking up at us, thinking surprised
as he must have been with his eyebrows raised that way, who are
these guys? as we take in the decor, taking our time
on the spruced-up spruce & polished, bright, unbevelled
mirrors & the hundred-watt-bulbed lights & the actually
almost smoke-free look & looking with a due disdain, saying
out loud & loud enough to raise the gaze of people sitting there,
'What is this awful place? What happened
to that pub that used to be here?' 'This
is horrible. I'll not be coming here
again.' And we let the doors swing back & left
the man with a look like his fork half-raised.

So much for the finger.

A PROMISE

When my sister was four,
my father made her promise
that she'd never grow any older.

I've always kind of liked him for that.

ELEGY
(for Dan Ferguson)

'On occasions we would exchange glances across a crowded room.
What did I see? A man trapped in his own decency, an artist of
distinction, a gentleman and my friend.'

Your death is there to make the worth
of colour, tone and emphasis —
when shadows fall, they never fall in black.

Light refracted shapes form substance: the vision of
Chagall. The bride and bridegroom rise in air
to darkness filled with stars.

— This morning on the telephone, John told me
you had died. And told me of
his Paris trip. The Matisse exhibition
was wonderful, of course — but it
wasn't that. His voice filled with the pleasure of
his visit to the Musée Rodin —
those enormous sculptures in the garden in
the open air — Balzac,
the Burghers of Calais: huge, the bronze itself
copious with life; but it wasn't that.
It was all above, a big blue sky,
and all around them, roses:
massive, standard roses, heavy and full
in bright red bloom, and the
sunlight lashing down on them,
on statues, flowers, his wife and him.
The shadows were everywhere.

Dan, stop my words.
Tonight for you, I'll think of all
the colours of the world, moving.

DONA NOBIS PACEM
(for Pamela)

You had no wish to leave this world and time
or us, but knew that in the way of things you would.
Without the indulgence of fancy, allow us to let you
go with the innumerable angels.

Not everyone can hear the things they need to
most, or tell them. I never had the chance
to tell you what I'd learned of Robert Carver —
voices in the vault of God, lifting, turning as a
film will take your eyes round corners
unsuspected, into naves and arches, liberated texts
of stone, cavernous cathedral space, pillars of sound supporting
the weight, rivers of voice, carrying rafts of us onward, on
parabolas of song: registers of penitence,
humility, and faith.

This morning at eight I heard you had died in the night,
at four. The lowest segment of the clock
closed in; night filled it, carried
the news to me, waking to the winter dawn.

At ten I played the six-part mass
and listened to it for you,
soaring, ascending, leaving us
things that are living
always so easily hurt.

> *Agnus Dei,*
> *qui tollis peccata mundi:*
> *miserere nobis; dona nobis pacem.*

COMMON LANGUAGE
— a memoir

July 31st

The phone call came just now. It sounds as though she is going down quickly. My parents and I talked about it for a few minutes. Her deterioration over the last week had been rapid.

It is a warm Tuesday afternoon in Kent. From the upstairs windows, you can see the London river, a milky, chalky blue over the roofs of the houses, and beyond it, Essex stretches northwards, pale green. We have to go now, we decided. My father said, 'This time we go jury-rigged.' It's a sailor's term for travelling light.

I'd arranged to meet a Caribbean novelist the next day. I cancelled; apologised. He responded at once, sympathetically, arranging an alternative, saying he hoped that I would not find the return visit too oppressive.

> There will have been these
> night-vigils; I remember them
> from when my grandfather lay there,
> in that bed, night after night.
> You take your watch, sitting,
> reading a book perhaps, attentive
> to any shift of breathing or the bedclothes
> when they fall; you perform the normal functions
> of whatever relation you are,
> if you get the chance.
> When the moment comes
> and there is no more breath upon the mirror,
> maybe it will seem that the pictures on the wall,
> the objects on the dressing table, everything
> hangs crucified, but it's over so
> suddenly you hardly notice at the
> time. No one is going into that room
> tonight, without, in some degree confronting
> the reality of a common language.

As I remember them, my grandfather's last words were a question.

He'd slipped into a coma, and came round again before dipping one more time, for good. 'For God's sake,' he said, simply annoyed, 'Am I still here then?'

The last thing I was told my grandmother said was when the doctor gave her an injection, to ease the pain. 'Is that better now?' one of my aunts asked her.

'That's lovely,' she said.

I'd been reading Adrienne Rich: 'If we could learn to learn from pain. . . .' And also, regret. I remember a girl from Lewis I knew once, her voice, coming down the phone, 'I am living with a little regret.'

There are these times that happen, and you can make mistakes.

It was a long drive north through a long summer evening in South Britain, the sun a perfect circle, violently gold, the cornfields turning blue and then grey and the sky becoming grey, then misty and pink. My father drives first. When it gets dark, I'll drive.

I was driving when we crossed the border, a few minutes after midnight. And on straight to the village. The streetlights only emphasize the dark. The narrow streets themselves are utterly empty; no lights show in windows. When we come to the small bungalow, the outside light is on and there are cars parked on the roadside there. Otherwise, there is no sign of life.

My grandmother had five sons and two daughters. Four of the sons were there, one with his wife; the younger daughter was asleep in the back bedroom, tired out. There was also a night nurse. In turns, we went into my grandmother's bedroom. She was comatose now, and had been since yesterday. You could see her breathing and hear her breathing. She was leaning back gently on a large pillow, her woollen bed-jacket pulled lightly around her shoulders.

Her breathing jumped a little and her eyebrows raised when an uncle spoke aloud to her, saying that we had arrived, naming us. It was very clear to see this when he named my mother, then again less powerfully, when he named my father, then powerfully again when he named me. You could see her body move in response; it seemed like recognition. I don't know. My uncle's wife told me she thought that she could hear us when we talked.

When we crossed the border, just after midnight, my mother had said to me, 'Happy birthday, Alan.' It was August 1st, 1990. I was 33.

I had thought she might have died while we were driving. So had both my parents, but none of us had said so. When we'd gone into the house, we didn't know. We were offered whisky but took tea, and after a cup I went back to the bedroom and sat beside the bed and held my grandmother's hand, or at least, laid my hand on it, a slight pressure and warmth.

Her hand was warm, firm. It didn't grasp, but squeezed from time to time.

I spoke to her, when no one else was in the room. I said that we were all here now, and that we loved her very much and that everything was all right now.

Then I sat on the chair beside the bed and said nothing for a long time, watching and listening to her breathe, and letting the warmth of my hand feel the warmth of hers.

One of my uncles said that when they were about to phone my mother, on Sunday, my grandmother asked him to speak before she took the telephone. That way, my mother wouldn't think it so strange when she didn't speak for very long. Then, he said, the change in her voice when he gave her the phone — its sudden infusion of strength as she spoke — surprised him. After she put the phone down, her voice could hardly be heard. He said that she was always thinking about the other person, never herself.

My grandmother was born on August 10th, 1902. She died at 3.20 a.m., about an hour after my parents and I had left the house to come into Glasgow. We'd all gone to bed; I was lying awake on the settee and heard the phone ring. When I heard that she had died I lay for a while, my eyes feeling water rise behind them.

On the first of May each year, for some part — perhaps most — of her life, she would wash her face in the morning dew. Some of her children remember doing that themselves.

The last time my mother saw her — just over a week ago — they played cards, sat, talked, spent time together, holding hands, sitting silently. When my mother asked her if she wanted anything — a cup of tea, some ice cream — she said no, she was just enjoying sitting there, with her, being there, together.

August 1st

It was warmer than I expected. Coming back out, the fields between Glasgow and the village were much greener than in Kent. It had been raining up here.

The big L-shaped nurse's pillow had been taken away, and she was rested against the pillows of her own bed.

By late afternoon the undertakers had been, and she was lying in her coffin in front of the big bookcase in the dining-room, the heavy oak table moved back to a corner, flowers on it. The lid on the coffin was three-quarters over her; the legend on the plaque read: 'Janet Cunningham / Died August 1st / 1990.'

Ten years ago, when my grandfather was dying, he had days of lying in bed, sometimes saying things, alluding to things we sometimes could not hear or understand. I remember him asking for soda water, quite urgently. He drank it with obvious pleasure, tasting it. Dry, dry water. He said he didn't want to leave this world thirsty.

Later, he was half-dreaming, he asked me: 'What was that poem? The better land. . .? Something about . . . the better land. It was by a woman. . . .'

I didn't know the poem. He'd never read it to me nor ever mentioned it before. I wondered if it would be in the big bookcase and went through to the dining-room to look for it.

The big bookcase is made of mahogany and glass: 8 feet tall and 7 feet wide. As a small child, one might almost literally have climbed into it. It had secret compartments. Most of the contents consisted of wonderful, huge, leatherbound volumes with titles like *Marvels of the Universe, Wonders of the World, Women of All Nations, Races of the World, Splendours of Art, The Casque of Literature*. There were encyclopaedias of sexual knowledge, dictionaries of biography, guides to world literature and the history of science. There was the blue and gold Border edition of Walter Scott, there were fine large-format volumes of Byron, Fielding, Keats, Shelley, Browning and Burns. There was the family Bible, a two-volume set of Boccaccio's *Decameron* with white leather spines and a few anthologies of Scottish poetry and song.

The only volume of poetry by a woman was a gilt-engraved, leather-bound, heavily embossed volume of Mrs Hemans, a popular Victorian sentimentalist.

I took her down and found the poem, sure enough. I read it out to him, sitting on a chair by the bedside. Other people were in the room.

By this time, his eyes were closed. He smiled in recognition when he heard it. 'Aye . . . aye . . .' he said.

When he died, my grandmother asked me to read the poem to the family, when they gathered for the service.

My mother told me that when she visited my grandmother, she found the typewritten copy I'd made of the poem near her, on the shelf beside her seat in the living-room. My mother said that she saw her lean over and take it down and read it silently to herself, and then put it back.

Early this morning, when she was living, when I was alone with her, sitting beside her, holding her hand, I thought of reading the poem to her, even though she was comatose. I remembered a few words, the first lines, and I whispered them out loud.

Again, as she had when we had said hello to her, when we arrived and were naming ourselves, she seemed to respond, her fingers moved, her eyebrows raised, a smile seemed to be forming on her face.

My parents are in the back room tonight; they've gone to bed.

Uncles and aunts have come and gone.

She is lying in her coffin in front of the big bookcase in the next room.

I am sleeping on the cushions of the settee in the living-room, where I have slept many times before. The air in this room is a thick, thick haze of stale cigarette smoke, ancient whisky-fumes, and memory's broken cloudbursts of half-forgotten speech.

And the house seems full of whispers, murmurs, quiet.

August 2nd

> you have to face
> the underside of everything you've loved —
> — Adrienne Rich

The morning is so warm, blue, cloudless. My mother has cleaned the bedroom of all the medicines. The curtains are drawn wide. Light fills every room, but one. The announcement will already have appeared in the *Glasgow Herald*.

In another village, when I was a young boy, my grandparents lived above a row of shops: a butcher's, a draper's, a co-operative. For a while, my grandfather had been the manager of the co-operative and they stayed in the apartments above it. These apartments were where my grandmother raised her children. For me they were a citadel of rooms, each with secrets, smells and textures of their own. Bookcases and cabinets with hidden panels, secret doors, furniture with different charms, the feel of a bed settee, an armchair with leather handrests, a radiogram with a big heavy lid that played 78s, as well as 33s and 45s.

Outside, there was a railed landing and the flat roofs and skylight of the co-op and behind that, a little lower, the flat roof of the milking shed. On the co-op roof, beside the skylight, my grandmother would hang out the washing. Sheets blowing on a clothesline: colours, sails.

Below, in the backyard, there were the stables. There were no horses there when I was a boy. One of my uncles kept pigeons in the stables, but he remembered the horses from his boyhood, when my grandfather took him out on the milk-carts, on deliveries.

And there was my grandfather's shed. He spent long evenings late into the night in there, working with wood. And there was a small garden, next to the wash-house. A narrow alley led between the wash-house and the stables to the plots, a triangular expanse of field, surrounded by farmland. From there you could see up to the farm on the horizon off to the right, while over to the left a row of council houses went marching down into the valley. Straight ahead, true west, the fields curved down through a copse of trees to the canal — a silver line snaked through trees, pitscapes, farmlands, towards the grey towers of Coatbridge, which you could see in the near distance. In the far distance, you could see the conurbation starting, Glasgow making the western sky at night a purple glow.

I have a distinct image of my grandmother, standing on that landing, as she would be seen had you been looking back from the plots, in an early summer evening twilight. Though she was not a small woman, she would be a small figure away up there in the distance, waving a teatowel and calling out 'Coo-ee!' — calling us up for our dinner or tea.

Last night one of my uncles asked, speaking to no one in particular, 'You remember Nana, when we were kids, she'd stand on the landing of the house back there, and call us up for our tea? She'd be waving a dishtowel?' He paused; he shook his head and took a puff of his cigarette. 'Gosh,' he said; 'it just seems like a hundred years ago.'

As if it was another life.

Thursday, early evening. I turn on the radio as I'm driving the car to the carwash at the garage and I'm hearing the last movement of Mahler's *Das Lied von der Erde*, the voice fading away on 'Ewig . . . Ewig. . . .'

And I have to smile at the timing of it, a smile like saying to myself, You know, you just can't escape from timing like that.

There is an aura, now, gathered in the room, of her command, of love. At one point when I went in with an uncle, to check the lamp, we found someone had put a light square of linen over her face, but we took it away, and she was there again, to be seen, to be beside, for a few moments, minutes.

When I was alone, standing beside her, I wanted to come forward and lean over her and kiss her forehead. I had wanted to do so yesterday evening, but did not. This time I did.

Her skin was smooth and curved and cold: beautiful marble. I touched her brow a moment with my lips and came away.

Aunts and uncles and cousins and other relations and family friends have come and gone again, throughout the evening.

My sister and her husband arrived up from London this afternoon. She shows her grief openly, quietly.

Nothing sounds tonight.

. . . A clock, somewhere. No murmurs, no more echoes of voices. The atmosphere has settled more quickly than it did last night, but it is still full.

This house will empty of us all, when we leave, as quickly as this.

The Kirk is on a windy hill in another part of Lanarkshire, above a different village, where my grandmother was born and grew up. She went to the Kirk as a child and young woman. She was married in the Manse, I heard today. Today at the place where the house she was born in used to stand, behind a fence, a tree grows. The house and the row of houses it was in are gone a long time ago. A small burn runs curving beside the tree, through grass. Below the Kirk, below and to the side of the long slope of the graveyard, a small well springs water, steel blue, ice cold and strong with iron.

August 3rd
The face I have seen changing for 33 years, I see today for the last time.

August 5th

Barefoot,
as a girl, running
in Lanarkshire hills
in 1910.

I telephoned the Caribbean novelist and told him what had hap-
pened, that my grandmother had died, that we arrived when we did,
on my birthday, and he asked if I remembered the lines, 'See, we are
born with the dead . . .' (which he used as an epigraph to one of his
novels). I did, and after I'd put the phone down, I found the book the
lines are quoted from, T. S. Eliot's *Four Quartets*, and looked at them
again:

We are born with the dead:
See, they return, and bring us with them.
The moment of the rose and the moment of the yew-tree
Are of equal duration. A people without history
Is not redeemed from time, for history is a pattern
Of timeless moments.

August 26th

Leaving the village, her house, this morning, it seemed for the last
time, I was impatient and wanted away. My father and I drive down
to Gravesend today. The car is packed: our cases, some of my grand-
mother's china, a giant scrapbook I once had made for me, big enough
to take a full page of newspaper, which I left behind the upright piano
in my grandmother's living-room. We're leaving my mother for two
further days on her own; her brothers and sister and brother- and
sisters-in-law all around her, to deal with last things, as she wished to.
   We're driving south.

North Essex.
   Grey with heat-haze, oppressively warm, with no gold about it,
grey, not as it was when we left to drive north, on the last day of July.
You cannot see the sun this afternoon for the haze. We're north of
Cambridge, a hundred miles from London. The yellowish fields are
dull, matt colours. At a glance it looks as though the harvest's ready,
but it's not. The grass is dried out, burnt out, everywhere you look.
   It hasn't rained properly at all, down here, all summer.

My father tells me the grass will turn green again very quickly, as soon as the rains begin again. But right now, it doesn't look too good.

We arrived at the Kirk after a half-hour drive through darkest Lanarkshire, past Ravenscraig, past Carfin Grotto, the Catholic shrine, and out along the motorway to the Kirk on the hill. Stark, black, overlooking the valley where the motorway runs, and a slate quarry, still working, the smoke trailing up from the sheds.

We had agreed that at some point the minister should break her sermon and ask me to read Mrs Hemans's poem.

The Kirk dates back to Covenanting times, with bulletholes still to be seen in the older gravestones, where armed nightwatchmen had opened fire on prospective bodysnatchers in the eighteenth and nineteenth centuries. It's cold and bleak and most days it's rainy and windswept and you can usually feel the cold of the wind and the rattle of the rain on the windows as you sit on the wooden pews. No wooden pew is soft, and these weren't even cushioned. Strangely enough, the people sitting there today did not look cold, and for once there seemed nothing bleak about the atmosphere. Yesterday had been warm and sunny — even up here — and a benevolent breeze freshened the air. Today it was raining — gently — in warm, mild, slowfalling showers, through warm air, so that the moisture dried as it touched your clothes.

When the time came, I got up from the third pew and walked out the waist-high swing door at the aisle, went up and onto the dais, carrying the leather gilt-edged copy of Mrs Hemans. I came to the lectern and putting the book of poems down on top of the open Bible there, I turned and faced them all.

Looking down I could hardly see the assembled company as a body of people, a mass, at all: there were individual faces I noticed, an uncle here, a distant relation there, a neighbour or acquaintance whose gaze moved to meet mine as I looked from one to another, not dwelling on any. Below, to my right, was the aisle I had just walked up. Below, to my left, the closed coffin.

'About ten years ago,' I said, 'My grandfather asked me to read him this poem. And it cheered him.'

I remember the tone of the word 'cheered': it was almost as if I was surprised to hear it.

Then I read the poem. It was hard work. When I was finished, I paused a moment and after a glance down at the coffin again, I said, 'I know that this is a public farewell to my grandmother.' And I raised my eyes and looked out not with my eyes but my whole face and body. 'But I know that I will be saying private farewells to them both for the rest of my life.'

Afterwards, the cortège drove around the hillside to the grave-yard. My sister and I walked down in the rain, down through the cemetery to the open grave, reaching it as the cortège was drawing up on the other side of the wall. The pallbearers carried the coffin over to the grave. Everyone gathered around.

They laid the coffin on the crossbars and coiled the eight purple ropes on the lid, then in turn each man's number was called by one of the undertakers. My eldest uncle, who had given us the small oblong cards, each carrying on one side a small diagram of the coffin and on the other our individual number, took the first position. I took the last.

The undertakers pulled away the crossbars underneath the coffin and in unison we lowered her, into the unfolded earth.

And then let the cords fall, softly and audibly, down.

Then backed away as the minister said some more words. And while most people had their heads bowed, I turned my face, looking up and out to the north, suddenly remembering that this was exactly what I had done nearly ten years ago, standing on the same spot. Today, I was doing the same thing again, but with no sense at all that it was merely repetition. I don't know what inner compulsion was at work that made me look in that direction.

Afterwards we backed away, left the place and drove back to the village. We dined in the village hotel, in the room to which we'd taken my grandmother for dinner about two months before. I remember her then, resplendently dressed, a white woollen stole over her shoulders, smiling, eating scampi in a white sauce, plainly enjoying herself, with eyes that still held their own activity, sipping a glass of white wine, sometimes slipping a little wine or sauce on the side of her mouth or her chin, not noticing it, and my eldest uncle, at the head of the table, taking his napkin to dab it off quickly, carefully, with a gentle accuracy.

After the funeral, we dined well, too: on thick tomato soup, roast beef and yorkshire pudding, potatoes, carrots, broccoli, a full, soft red wine, and strawberries and cream to follow.

I found myself sitting at the top table, with my parents, my eldest uncle and his wife, and the minister.

From time to time I couldn't help lapsing into silence.

At one point the minister mentioned my grandmother's knowledge of local traditions and folklore. She said it was interesting because it had been raining at the cemetery during the funeral. It was strange that it should have been raining today, she said, after all that summer warmth and sunshine. She told me it reminded her of the saying that if it rained at your funeral, you'd go to your rest content.

'Ah well,' I said smiling at her, pleased by this and thinking of the weather. Everyone at the table was thinking the same thing, including the minister herself. It had to be said with a smile: 'There must be a lot of happy people in your graveyard.'

The Dartford Tunnel. 70 pence.

As we approach the sloping road that will take us under the Thames, we look over at the enormous bridge being built, further east. This vast construction extends from either side, north and south, but each side hangs in air, suspended on tall, lean concrete pillars.

The M2. Gravesend, a mile ahead. The sun's come through the heat haze, burning low.

Everything looks slanted, moving, now, a tilted field. A Chinese mouse rests on the dash. Good luck. Fast cars.

Egyptian light.

My father says, 'This could be Mars.'

August 28th

A Tuesday. Four weeks exactly, since this began. My father and I picked up my mother at Euston, and we drove back to Gravesend again together. I went into the employment office this afternoon, to explain why I hadn't signed on last week.

'I had to go to Scotland,' I said. 'My grandmother died. I had to be in Scotland for the funeral.'

The woman stands there looking at me through her glasses with the kind of blank expression you might find only in a place like this, and she says, 'Well, if it happens again you'll have to fill out a holiday form.'

THE BETTER LAND

"I hear thee speak of the better land,
Thou callest its children a happy band;
Mother, oh! where is that radiant shore?
Shall we not seek it, and weep no more
Is it where the flower of the orange blows,
And the fireflies glance through the myrtle boughs?"—
    "Not there, not there, my child!"

"Is it where the feathery palm-trees rise,
And the date grows ripe under sunny skies?
Or 'midst the green islands of glittering seas,
Where fragrant forests perfume the breeze,
And strange, bright birds, on their starry wings,
Bear the rich hues of all glorious things?"
    "Not there, not there, my child!"

"Is it far away in some region old,
Where the rivers wander o'er sands of gold?—
Where the burning rays of the ruby shine,
And the diamond lights up the secret mine,
And the pearl gleams forth from the coral strand?—
Is it there, sweet mother, that better land?"—
    "Not there, not there, my child!"

"Eye hath not seen it, my gentle boy!
Ear hath not heard its deep songs of joy;
Dreams cannot picture a world so fair—
Sorrow and death may not enter there;
Time doth not breathe on its fadeless bloom,
For beyond the clouds, and beyond the tomb—
    It is there, it is there, my child!"

— Mrs Felicia Hemans

2   Difficult Matter

I too have heard the dead singing.

And they tell me that
This life is good
They tell me to live it gently
With fire, and always with hope.
There is wonder here

And there is surprise
In everything the unseen moves.

— Ben Okri, 'An African Elegy'

The whole thing it is, the difficult
matter: to shrink the confines
down. To signals, so that I come
back to this. . . .

— J. H. Prynne, 'The Numbers'

THAT SILENCE

I kept thinking of that silence we fell into,
sometime after the shower, it seemed the last,
when every touch was wanting more, denied
and every time we held
                    each other, we held on
time; and of, when I held you then, so
close, looking over your shoulder, as we were
dressed and standing by your suitcase by the door
looking back on that great broad bed,
its white sheets tumbled, broken into Alps —
and I've been thinking too about the way, then,
we moved away so quick,
                    and the way
I could say nothing; and neither could you —

that silence that we let ourselves fall into —

so that now, we can break it again.

THE OTTER
(for L. and M. J.)

Thinking of the otter, the sea-otter, that had dipped, in Skye, near Elgol, once,
in the slip of the channel, built for boats, that I did not see
— it had gone down before, at the call of others, I raised my eyes —
I thought back to your high windows, overlooking
that long windswept beach near Dunedin
(as if, in California, in winter)
along which, like something seen through a telescope, from a
play by Jack B. Yeats, the hacks and horses
raced, solitary,
as the big grey waves crashed whitening on the sand
and washed up the strand
while the clouds curled over like fingernails.

I was thinking only of
something I missed
and think of it now, only because
in this airless car in the baking heat on a Sunday
afternoon, on a road heading south from
Coromandel, I think I'm going to fall
asleep, and don't want to,
or want to
miss
anymore.

THE TREATY

Nothing corrects
the haircracks in the crockery.
No patina on skin
could cure the open traces or the branches of our blood.

THE EAST CAPE

'Since then I have questioned no further'

i
'language is the hawk' / driving the car
I'm coiled above / no reasons
oblivion, eternity, this see-
saw scene, is politics, the lot
of common men and women. Dark
mountains casting shadows and the lowering clouds,
an overcast junta of hills, sulphurous rivers,
Saturday afternoon rugby matches, crowds
at every village hall and rugby field
and orchards. Here is the late fruit
of a chill autumn. Here are gulfs and caves
in cold volcanic rock. Here are inexplicable
fissures. The horror of mistakes in common ground, or seasons
or simply how what men and women are.

ii
The day passed like a bad old jerky film
black and white, Saturday
mainly afternoon.
Evening sent perpendicular
shafts of awful pink across
the long, dimensional clouds, over
the beach. White Island smoked
on the horizon. The horizon all day
had been a dark grey cut,
sharp and clean as a thing
could be, like coffee
or an American
lightness, a final
farewell, a last sense
of things not done, that never will
be done, because there are these things,
these other things, to do.

iii

. . . the morning after Saturday
Opotiki reunion meeting, we left the streets swept clean of litter,
the terraced colonial hotels, the bars with their high heavy fans,
that yellow beer, and crossed the bridge, drove into the green
again, and faced the hills, the unconverted
forest and the sea. Despite what's seen is spectacle
at every turn, the curve slips further, the long horizon
angles out of sight —
the constant and the common pain
of a simple, slight dyspepsia, acid working in belly and bowel
forbodes that what we're coming to might be
the first place in the world,
'at the dawn's pink kiss'; but what we get
is inanition, tea with milk, and
television programmes about spies.

iv

Legacies of emptiness, swinging the car
at night on the dock road, headlights turning
past the carpark by the yacht club, where a
young couple are locked in a clinch, his
hands upon her head,
return, slowly driving past the freezing-works by the fishing boats.
The gluttonous mouth of the place takes in
every building gesture made towards true avowal, leaves you
human pain.
Races go down like shells in sand, like mist,
like cannibal air, like eaten gods
leaving only a tree
that knows death
or a cave or a cemetery held
forever in the long, long corridors,
the coral of your mind.
So much moves over distance like a draught
blowing down
the telephone, with all the questions there are
unanswered.

HOLMES

With your fingertips resting gently upon
        your fingertips, anyone's
fingers seem long; his gaze
slides over from the unoccupied chair, across
        the fixed steel fender and the fire
of glowing coals, to the Persian
slipper tobacco-pouch
        and behind the eyes the tumblers
fall exactly,
        precise as pigeons
you cannot explain
        crossing the most immense
distances, with a simple fall, a turn
of phrase, of thought, of a realised train
of motion,
of, towards all, behind a steady glance
and only that, between the gulf and the scuttle
keeps you from

That, and the habits of the day.

GOING UNDER THE BRIDGE
(after César Vallejo)

the words connect before they are real words
I gather what I think I need to guide them then and wait
I feel as though I'd want to write and want to write and wait

— You're sitting on the port bow, waiting
returning towards the anchorage,
going under the bridge where the winds drop,
and it's like that, there, when you want to say so much,
when the sails are full of a guiding wind and suddenly
the wind drops
       the bridge
is above you —

               you cannot speak precisely of
               co-ordinates that mean
               the wind will drop exactly
               there, no other place
               or when. Nothing computes
               as exactly
               as that.
               Cross-winds and currents, too
               impossible to guess —

You feel as though you'd want to write and want to write and wait
You feel as though there is so much you want to say and wait

THE ACCENT
(after César Vallejo)

The accent hangs from my shoe
heard perfectly, amber and tenacious,
an outsize mischievous shadow
watching me go forward —
while the judges sit in the trees
like monkeys, watching me go forward —
shrugging my shoulders
into the sound of the hammer
striking the wood!
        (There's no one beside me,
        of course, & they've all
        said I should go.
The accent, suddenly
big in the elastic fog,
with quickness above & from & by,
makes all the prophetic telephones
ring!

THE FINAL WORD ON VEGETARIANS
(Lester's poem)

'My old dad sacked a man once
because he was a vegetarian.
He told us straight out, he said —
My mum said, What do you eat?
He said, Oh, eggs. I eat eggs,
and vegetables. Eggs? said my
dad. Yeah, I'll eat eggs.
Not if the rooster's been near them,
said my old dad. No. No, no.
No, no, no. I can't work a man
who doesn't eat. You can
pack your swag. That's
what he said. Have you ever seen
a nest of hawks, of baby hawks?
They lie on their backs with their claws in the air
and swear at you, you know. Yeah. You can
have a lot of fun with them, you know.
Well, that vegetarian found a nest of them
and killed them with a shovel. Yeah.
Skinny bastard. I never saw a hawk kill anything,
you know. Other than rabbits, and small birds
they'll take, but that's how it is,
for them. The worst of them, I think,
are those black-backed gulls. They'll go
for the sheep. Start with the afterbirth, and
one thing leads to another, you know. Its eyes, its
tongue; then the other end. Yeah, life's hard
where they come from. That bastard.'

CARNIVOROUS PICKUP, LA

Los Angeles: Stop
over, London to
New Zealand,
walking with
the others, tourists,
on the path
beside the road,
on the edge
of the sheer
cliff dropping
down to the
beach below, my
father sd he
noticed, saw a
wee mouse or a
vole or something
furry come up
out of the grass
on the lip of
the cliff, & thought
to himself, look! when a
bolt fell out of the blue, a hawk, & was gone with it, so
swiftly hardly
anyone had seen it & they
all were walking on, as it
happened, above the beach where the surf breaks up in big white
    rollers onto a strip
of strand where a beachhouse now marks the spot
of a Kennedy/Marilyn tryst.

AT ARROWHEAD
(for Ward Kirchwehm)

i
Driving into Mass., last night,
the sky ahead was Ulysses with sheets
of lightning, rigging cracks
of searing light, come down
like jagged ligatures, to touch.
The rain came down the moment when
we crossed the stateline
to the other side: like
waves that crash upon the bridge, on
glass you're looking out from,
driving ahead with, into the storm.

ii
At Arrowhead,
the centre
of a still and turning storm,
imagination's vortex turned to weather, actual, sore:
skin rubbed raw from handling the shrouds
bush-rope, buoy-tow, voice
grown hoarse with shouting
over wind-cracked canvas, croaking wood —
muscles flayed with swimming,
trying to reach the island —
collapsed into the lea
of white New England linen, consigned to dream
of Ishmael
or nightmare,
drenched and done and trembling on the beach —
the sheets salt into sweat
& break up, into waves —

You started the hunt that tracks us,
even now —

iii
Even now,
at Arrowhead,
the judgement of the mountain is its distance
— implacable. The forest runs
from your designed piazza on
up into the mountains, round them, on to
the Atlantic.

At Arrowhead, a chimney & its hearth, a roof —
a life of domesticity & debt.
You called it Damned in Paradise
visited by ghosts —
            one of 'the dark characters'
writing truths (to utter them, 'all but madness' —

Poking the coals in the fire with a half-harpoon.

From height to height, the language rises to
articulate a silence we cannot break past.

iv   The Picnic
Melville on the summit of the mountain,
looking over Pittsfield, Lenox, Adams,
looking back, at Arrowhead,
the forest stretching, rushing
forward, beating round him, waving. The dark,
dramatic cloud comes down in heavy weighted
sheets of grey: matt, portentous, loomings. He is
driven, raising his arms in his shirt-sleeves,
hauling on imaginary hawsers,
seeing the ropes come down from the empty sky from
God, and calling to the sailors on the yard-arms and
the deck-hands down below to
put those baskets down, to get aloft.
His silent scream's still gulping down the air.

THE CANYON

Here the air has overgrown all your American gods.
All eagles drown in silence here. This most
grandiloquent thing puts paid to all the air you breathe
against the drop, this measured, immense, curved
stratification: blue sky arced above gold
earth, and river blue, a threaded line, below:
       a sequence of unnumbered bows,
       held in coil by empires of the
       Odyssean air. The Abyss, the length
       of one footstep
       away, and miles of it across,
       and in it, millions of unthinkably
       intricate forms: a poem far too
       complex ever to read. This is
       the final library of congress.
(Every itemed throw of dice or turn of card
ever made in Vegas, noted for a meaning,
turned into a story here
that interweaves
with others.)
       If a library at
       night is a sleeping monster,
       all the monsters of the world
       are measured and located
       in its depths. All dictionaries
       fall and tumble up from
       it. Whatever your own worst
       memory is, be it shameful
       and embarrassing, a regret you
       have daily and live with,
       the grief you caused,
       your carried hurt, whatever
       pains you, measure it against
       this. It is the fact that it displays
its stories, makes detailed accounts of all
its evidence, that allows you
to measure yourself alongside it

in a human way, glad at last
to recognise your own attempts
are only and ever
exactly these, and to be
of the company of those whose
attempts have also been made.
      All words sink and
      seep in this; all creatured things
      stand back, balance
      as they can. The air blots out
      all words we ever write in it,
      is merciful, to turn us back.

THERE AND YOU ARE

There and you are. Inside this place again. Beyond
the window-frame, the sea, and over there, Ord.

On the shin-high uncemented stone slab wall, a lobster-pot;
to its left, a ram's skull; a smaller skull to the left of that and

thrusting its old white fingers like thorns, to the left of that,
there's a crooked, bare, weigelia shrub, entangled beyond the window to

an elder tree. The grass between the wall and the house
comes right up under the window and I'm writing this on the marble slab

of the kitchen table-top, on which as well the coffee in its bowl is
steaming, the gas lamp stands on the *West Highland Free Press*

and the *Glasgow Herald*. There's the butter dish, the cheese in its
crockery, the salt and pepper: they've been there since breakfast time.

It's noon. The light suffuses the mist away out there,
across that broad bright arm of water, and comes in over

here, sings cool in this room, in its peat smells, the fire
in the stove, as if the smell pervades the light, and hesitates.

There, again. In January. There are echoes still from the room upstairs
of hammering of nails in wood; birdsong from the elder tree outside;

and that weigelia, so I'm told, although it puts out no leaves now
will blossom into flower again come summer.

GONE FISHING

It was a grey, bright, sullen, jagged, tumultuous sky,
thick with light over the spars and jambs of wood,
diagonal constructions, platforms, cross-bars and struts
like the trestle of a railway bridge, like something
on a building-site but bigger, reaching out
(without a trace of disappointment) over the grey,
bright, turning, flowing, flat, somnambulant Tyne.

We stood among the wooden spars and sleepers,
grazing our touch on huge iron bolts; we fished
the river, the line long and heavy from this great height,
casting out in a vast arc over the air, watching the line,
watching the weight at the end of it, and the bait, the lugworm, fall,
a dull flash at the end of a long parabola.
And the line ran swiftly along my fingers, along the rod.

The flatties and the flounders that pulled on the line seemed muscular,
heavy, with a clotted, sandy grey in them, heavier in the air, absurdly
swinging, swaying, as we took turns, pulling them out of the river
and up to our perch, hoping they wouldn't slounge off, bodies flapping
down again to the river. There wasn't much more to it
than that. We took enough back for your grandmother to turn
into something white as cloud can be, flaky and rich,
battered in crisp gold, and served with thick chipped potatoes,
dappled with vinegar, sprinkled with salt. And good.

LATE SPRING: MORNING

The time has come, the Walrus said, it's blue
as a Millport afternoon out there and *warm*,
for a change. Cimarron is late today, but
he'll come. The rain has suddenly stopped. So,
with a diet Coke and a tin (of Royal Game Soup),
we're on for Pleasure — to get what it gives. Oh,
Sleepyhead. Junked foolscap. Cakes and Ale.
Ale? Where, here? I thought not. Call me
Bluebottle, bogomil or stare. I'll not be
overdone. Zeugma is used after more than
a litre. And you won't pass muster or even
St Peter. But let's get dressed anyway. Be suave.

3   Another Life

Recuerdas cuando
en invierno
llegamos a la isla?
Habitaste la casa
que te esperaba oscura
y encendiste las lámparas entonces.

[Do you remember when
in winter
we reached the island?
You occupied the house
that darkly awaited you
and then you lit the lamps.]

— Pablo Neruda, *The Captain's Verses*

ANOTHER LIFE
(for Rae)

As if the answers came out like ready replies
As if you did not know that sleeplessness
As if your smile had not been sent
As if there was not humour in the oboe
    I never felt the wind stir leaves like this
    or a bird, sing, hear that, over
    percussion's Tintagel
    dreamsongs, hush
    puppies, a cat
    quiet as a
    & you,
falling into comfort, a kind
of comfort like a shoe in a shoebox
& I, telling consolations by the shore.

A POEM ABOUT FOUR FEET

Last night, my two feet
lay on each other, warm as toast
in my single bed, between clean sheets,
till I rose, padded over
the New Zealand wool carpet to
the kitchen linoleum, sat down
at the table, and wrote
about your two feet in your socks,
tramping somewhere north of the equator,
in the middle of my night.
I was thinking of how my two feet
had lain there sleeping,
folded, like cats, twitching,
wondering, where your two feet,
which wanted them to play with,
were. And how they would have been
so much happier
sleeping near to each other,
four familiar feet,
hard, soft and warm,
in a single bed
somewhere, with you, alone.

THE BALANCE

For all the days my mother's mother spent
silent with her husband's obstinate pride — an
inordinate man, in a small, recalcitrant country,
where that kind of life is daily,

     I'd want to mention love,
   that means you're sleeping now
        in the room
right next to this one;

       Ronald Center's hushed
      Dona Nobis Pacem is
helping me remember

       the simple aspiration of
        Andrei Rublyov —

   and the thought of all intensity
  swings back: he would
  have understood
  the stubbornness that made
  a film like that, an icon,
     love, a bell.

THE PROMISE
(Prothalamium)

A tall lass looking forward to
her wedding day,
              as dusk falls
cool, beneath the falls,
in Whangarei,
              dreams
yesterdays'
tomorrows stay
in falling trails. . . .

They turn all white
to chestnut, and all
streams turn to flow; and
she falls
          back from a
              past
            into
the futures we shall know
and smiles within
December dusk,
this evening's summer light:
and promises
late day forever,
now
against the night.

SLEEPERS AWAKE
(Epithalamium)

The road is a straight diagonal line
a crooked corner takes it from sight in the distance
under the rough horizon of the nearer hills
and the higher serration of the range beyond; beside the road
to the right, in the lower triangle
of the big square window-frame, a chestnut mare is running
(essence of horse, racing itself in its paddock)
'the fields in view' are clear, green defined
by unobtrusive fences, and maybe young oak trees
(looking light as gossamer from here)
by the driveway of a white house by the roadside, marking one
boundary of home; to the left, above the top of
the pohutukawa trees, just below our view, another
triangle of rough scrub bogs out past a copse
of dark-leaved macrocarpa trees
to a long spit of mangrove-covered land, stretching
across arcs of sandy beach and small grassy islanded bays,
into the large, calm, cradling bay of the sea, and the mussel beds,
off to our left.

        The lower slopes of the hills ahead
are riach land, a whole hillside
of native bush, dark green bushes
and light green grasses, banks of bushes,
of mottled shades, of brindled colour,
sapling strokes of silver birch.

        And over us,
over the roof of the house,
over our bed
the sky is blue,
the clouds in view
move lightly, steady, weightless —
like serious but gentle
ministers of state

compacted in a government of order, in which
all things conspire, to make this celebration.

      Birdsong persists through the long, cool sounds
of occasional cars and trucks that pass
on the road (west-coast peninsular).
We're here. The cock-crow dawn of gentle and sedately
moving morning rises into blue and white, to the rooster's
firy flame-flap wattle, and the turkeys gobbling bagpipe waddle;
starling, blackbirds, finches, dipping in
the water-tanks for a drink, swallows skimming, magpies,
and a song you heard in your childhood or youth
from a bird out there whose name no longer knows us.
The love-song of the thrush, maybe. Heralds of the morning.
Their cage is all the world, and so are we.

COROMANDEL, 14/9/92

NECESSITY OF LISTENING
(for John Purser)

Love makes belief in miracles,
and future brings its own time, not the past's
predictions. You're right enough,
John: we should be content, contented.

Today, your new boat rests
in chuckling water, moored near Glasgow.
Soon you will take her to Skye.
Your hand will rest and move upon the tiller.

Tonight, my wife: her hand upon my arm
now knows no source for its resting;
her sleeping smile is unknowing as I am;
her comfort content is my own, her husband.

URLAR

It's one of those sodden, Sunday afternoons
in a wet New Zealand winter: everything is green
and soaked right through. The bush falls
over itself down on the walls of the garden.
I'm listening to bagpipes, another explanation of
the origins of pibroch: the human voice, and
all the limitations of the actual instrument.
It will return to the ground-bass, or urlar.
I'm thinking of elsewhere, another ground, Rachmaninoff,
and a drone of feeling fear that cold and wet
will raise blue mould on spines of books, of
relatively worthless books: my grandfather's collection —
the works of S. R. Crockett. The nature of inheritance.
That fear. There is another urlar playing now,
sounding with the surge of waves. Scotland
might seem not so far but near; surely
there's as much rain here. And music.

MATERIAL OF DREAM
(after Wilson Harris)

She is flesh-and-blood in my dream
of light, created, her creation is this.
Cry of a bird in a rainswept garden.
Vague outlines of egg, sea, silence, sound:
drawn on the curtains at the window.
Deep-seated sun, crystal music, glass, fossil fire —
the patter of rain on the street outside the window.

I was flying in my sleep. Your flesh
and blood have swallowed the sun and you rise
with the dark smile of love now thick with the wetness
of lips, that are prayers, prayed by the thighs,
bruised apples, wheat or corn or something darker
than wine, the prayer of the flood, the art
of the foetus.
          These are the newly created economies
of flesh-and-blood. The half-embrace of swimming
centuries, our selves invested with landscapes
and histories: the old dream, where populations hide,
masked in your beauty, the savage art we practise,
the bright blood on your body:
a drama of unfathomable innocence,
bone to bone, bruise to bruise. 'It is as if
you are in me and I in you forever.'
A pointed rain. A pointed rainlessness. 'We are
in each other's immaterial supports, bodies
in curious combat, reconciled. . . .' She
listened, heard everything, knew it
all; she heard, nothing, she hummed a silent tune
of these material and immaterial illuminations;
laughed gently now at him; he laughed, they
reached through space as if he were two persons,
orphans of sun, one red, one gold. He held her
in loving fear in fear in love, fabulously vulgar,
mad in curves and angles, fearfully strong and lastingly
it seemed and made as if for all

circumnavigational seasons of the body
and the world. 'And I give him a miracle. Yes
I do.' Laughing gently still as that first night,
and light fell as various disguises upon them:
a feathered stone that could not float or sink,
a blanket, an animal pool, at which one drank with a beak,
sensitive as the tongue of an angel.

The lake grows light within the room
swelling from the window,
                          attunes itself to the ticking clock,
the swishing of the curtains, turning wheels outside
of cars and flying fins of dolphins swimming
Mozart somersaults outside, in the rainswept air
of the city. The cool feathered flute and the glint
of your lips. The waterfall. The Fall of Coul.
Wings in the sea. My lips bend down to you.

My thirst is undying in the chorus of earth.
An undying hunger I have in the chorus of sky.
And here is grain. And here is seed.

They loved and slept again.

Notes

FROM FLINDERS, SOUTH AUSTRALIA, DRIFTS ANOTHER SCENT OF DISTANCE

The Clanline was a Scottish cargo-liner shipping company, sometimes known as the Scottish Navy, as at one time it had the largest number of ships of any shipping company. It survived from the 1880s to the 1970s. Clanline ships were distinct in having a black funnel with two red bands and a red house flag with lion rampant. The Clanline was eventually amalgamated with the Union Castle Line and became the British and Commonwealth Shipping Company. Clanline ships ran mainly out of Glasgow, Liverpool and London, to ports in India, Africa and Australia. The 'lascars' were Indian sailors. A 'howe' is a hollow.

A SHORT INTRODUCTION TO MY UNCLE JOHN

The epigraph, roughly translated, means: 'No verses can please or live long that are written by water-drinkers.'

ELEGY

Dan Ferguson (1925–1993). Glasgow artist and teacher. The epigraph is from a personal tribute by David Donaldson.

DONA NOBIS PACEM

Robert Carver (1484/5–after 1568) was a churchman and composer of polyphonic (many-voiced) Roman Catholic music for the King's Chapel in pre-Reformation Scotland. Two motets and at least five settings of the Mass survive and have recently been performed (and recorded) for the first time since the Reformation. Carver may also have been involved in the architectural design and building of the church where some of his compositions would have received their first performances. 'Agnus Dei . . .' — 'Lamb of God, that takest away the sins of the world: have mercy upon us; grant us Thy peace.'

THE EAST CAPE

The epigraph comes from the Sibelius orchestral song of the same name, 'Se'n har jag ej frågat mera' (Opus 17:1). The text is by Johan Ludwig Runeberg, and is variously translated as 'And I questioned them no further' or 'Afterwards I asked no more'. The phrase 'language is the hawk' is from the novelist Janet Frame: 'I feel that language in its widest sense is the hawk suspended above eternity, feeding from it but not of its substance and not necessarily for its life and thus never able to be translated into it; only able by a wing movement, so to speak, a cry, a shadow, to hint at what lies beneath it on the untouched, undescribed almost unknown plain.' (*Living in the Maniototo*, London & Auckland: The Women's Press/Hutchinson Group, 1981, p.43.)

GOING UNDER THE BRIDGE

This poem is not in any sense a translation of the Peruvian César Vallejo (1892–

1938). It arises from a small number of words and phrases in one of Vallejo's poems, 'Intensidad y altura', which begins, 'Quiero escribir, pero me sale espuma' ('My want is to write but what I produce is spume, foam-bells').

THE ACCENT
Like the preceding poem, this is not intended as a strict translation of Vallejo, although it roughly follows the structure of his poem, 'El acento me pende del zapato . . .'

THE FINAL WORD ON VEGETARIANS
This is a more or less exact transcription of the spoken words of Mr Lester Ashby-Peckham, and is published with his generous permission.

THE BALANCE
Ronald Center (1913–1973) was a composer of considerable distinction, undeservedly neglected. The cantata *Dona Nobis Pacem* is a haunting work, a record of spiritual doubt yet also a statement of commitment and faith, foreshadowing Britten's *War Requiem*. It has recently been recorded. Andrei Rublyov or Andrei Rublëv (*c.*1370–*c.*1430) was a Russian icon painter whose life and passion became the subject of a film written and directed by Andrei Tarkovsky (1932–1986). The film, made in black-and-white and colour, was released in the USSR in 1966 and took the International Critics Award at Cannes in 1969. It presents a harrowing series of interconnected stories and epiphanies in the life of the artist. The last episode culminates in the construction of a copper bell by a young boy whose life depends on the success of the operation. See *Russian Icons* by David Talbot Rice (London & New York: King Penguin, 1947) and *Andrei Rublëv* by Andrei Tarkovsky (London, Faber & Faber, 1991).

SLEEPERS AWAKE
The title is from Bach; 'the fields in view' and 'the sky is blue' are phrases from Burns's song, 'Now Westlin Winds' otherwise known as 'Song, composed in August', in Burns's *Poems and Songs*, edited by James Kinsley (London: Oxford University Press, 1969, pp.2–3).

URLAR
S. R. Crockett (1859-1914) wrote over 50 books, all of which were very popular during his lifetime. *The Stickit Minister* (1893) and *The Lilac Sunbonnet* (1894) are sentimental small-town tales of the 'Kailyard' school, while *The Raiders* (1894) and *The Men of the Moss-Hags* (1895) are historical adventures set in his native Galloway. *Mad Sir Uchtred of the Hills* (1894) is probably one of his worst.

MATERIAL OF DREAM
This poem is largely (but not entirely) a verse transcription from the prose of Wilson Harris, cf. his novel *Da Silva da Silva's Cultivated Wilderness* (published with *Genesis of the Clowns* in one volume, by Faber & Faber, 1977); see especially pp.4–6. The poem is published with the kind approval of Wilson Harris. The Fall of Coul is the highest waterfall in Scotland.